STRING

STRING

TYING IT UP
TYING IT DOWN

JAN ADKINS

CHARLES SCRIBNER'S SONS • NEW YORK

Maxwell Macmillan Canada • Toronto

Maxwell Macmillan International • New York • Oxford • Singapore • Sydney

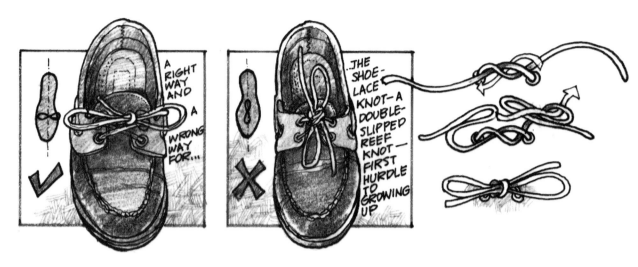

Copyright © 1992 by Jan Adkins

Charles Scribner's Sons Books for Young Readers
Macmillan Publishing Company, 866 Third Avenue, New York, NY 10022

Maxwell Macmillan Canada, Inc.
1200 Eglinton Avenue East, Suite 200, Don Mills, Ontario M3C 3N1

Macmillan Publishing Company is part of the Maxwell Communication Group of Companies.

First edition   10 9 8 7 6 5 4 3 2 1
Printed in the United States of America

Library of Congress Cataloging-in-Publication Data
Adkins, Jan.
    String : tying it up, tying it down / Jan Adkins. — 1st ed.   p.   cm.
    Summary: Discusses the many uses of string, rope, line, and knots, from rigging sails and clotheslines to tying packages and sewing buttons.
    ISBN 0-684-18875-9
    1. String—Juvenile literature.   2. Knots and splices—Juvenile literature.
[1. String.]   I. Title.
TS1785.A35 1992   677'.71—dc20
                                                                            91-25786

To my children:
SALLY and SAM

Fathers have seldom needed their children as much as I have, seldom leaned on them for as much support. They gave me more love and more strength than I asked for. I love them, but, more, I admire them.

The Opening Line

String. You know string as well as I do. It has a nasty mind of its own, and it is one of the few nonliving things that can be insulting. You can coil it, roll it, wind it neatly, and put it in a dark drawer; when you need it, the wicked stuff slithers out like left-over spaghetti, but tougher.

String is too short or too long. It loops around the pencil jar when you are pulling a little more to wind around a package and the pencils scatter, rolling off the table just ahead of the jar, which would break if it didn't hit the dog,

and the dog leaps up barking but one paw is caught in the hateful string and your package—the collection of birds' eggs you were trying to wrap—makes a small crunching sound as it hits the floor as the dog stumbles against the TV cart, which has snared the string that had lassoed the jar-struck dog, and the cart rolls, trailing string, over the sill of the basement door and down the steps, bouncing and crashing, trailing the egg collection and the wide-eyed, frantically barking, string-wound dog, and finally there is an explosion as the TV hits the concrete basement floor, knocking over a ladder, which hits the fuse box and the lights go out and when the firefighters come they find you standing on the porch trying to unravel string.

You know string.

The Party Line

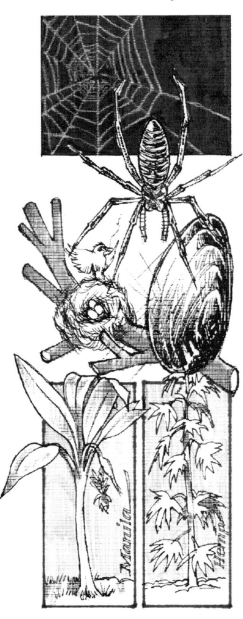

String, line, rope, warp, hawser, cable . . . It's all the same thing: something you can pull but can't push.

A mussel, clinging to its rock under the tumbling waves, produces thin fibers called byssuses that anchor it home. These fibers form the "beard" of the mussel and run out of the shell to sticky anchoring points.

Spiders are more sophisticated line workers; they produce the thinnest wisp of a fiber many times stronger than steel. Climbing, tugging, swinging from their own lines, they construct a tension structure across a wind current like fishermen trail a net across ocean currents. Made of two silks—dry to climb on and sticky to catch with—it has the strength and stretch to survive wind and the struggle of doomed bugs, which will be paralyzed by venom and bound alive in silk for a late dinner.

Birds have no fibers of their own, so they must use what is available: springy grasses, tattered palm fibers, reed bits, anything they can find. They twist and fasten them into nest patterns written by all of the birds of their kind before them.

People, too, use what they can. Wherever they have settled, they have found a fiber strong enough for their uses. By beating and soaking plants, they separated fibers from soft pulp. They washed and combed them to arrange the strength of the fibers in one direction. For thousands of years men and women have twisted the *fibers* into long *yarns*. They made a *strand* by twisting many yarns in the opposite direction; the friction between the threads kept the strand together. With three strands twisted together in the original direction, they made a three- or four-strand *line*. Fibers that decayed easily were twisted up with tar or beeswax for strength and rot resistance, like the tarred marline and waxed sail-twine that sailors still use.

Look at a piece of line closely: The individual fibers aren't twisted as much as the telling makes it sound. The beautiful structure of this ancient invention allows each strong fiber to lie almost straight along the lines of tension.

Today, we make fibers for our specific needs out of nylon, Dacron, polypropylene, and polyethylene. Fibers that can be miles long are twisted or braided in complex weaves to offer us our choice of colors, strength, stretch, floatability. We still have three-strand rope, though, in Manila or synthetic fibers, and twines made from cotton and jute still wrap up cardboard cartons or bunches of spruce seedlings.

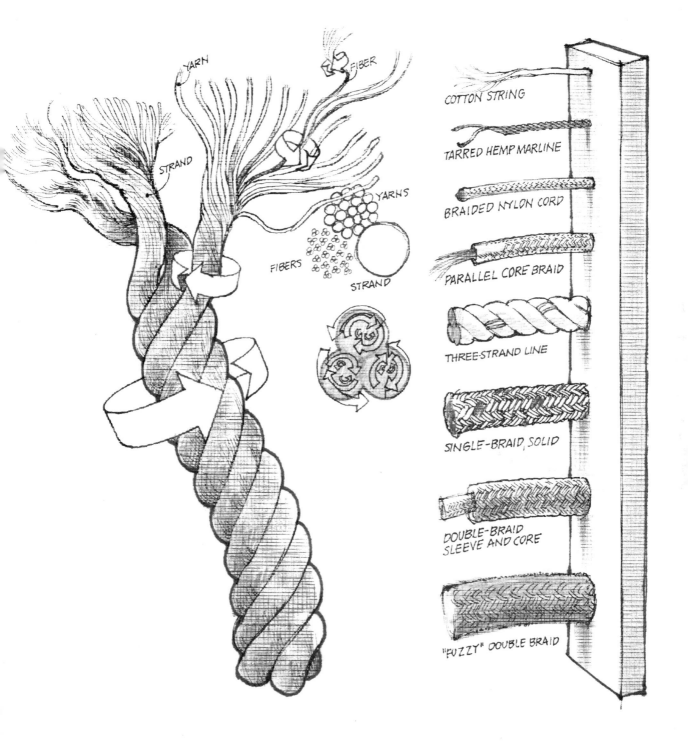

YARN

FIBER

STRAND

YARNS

FIBERS

STRAND

COTTON STRING

TARRED HEMP MARLINE

BRAIDED NYLON CORD

PARALLEL CORE BRAID

THREE-STRAND LINE

SINGLE-BRAID, SOLID

DOUBLE-BRAID
SLEEVE AND CORE

"FUZZY" DOUBLE BRAID

The Tie That Binds

A large part of the world is held together with strings.

Our clothes are woven from strings of cotton, wool, silk, linen, and polyester, then sewn together with fine thread. The Golden Gate Bridge spans 4,200 feet between San Francisco and Marin County on steel strings. Eye surgeons, belly surgeons, and veterinarians close up their clients with delicate knots in thin, strong string. Itzhak Perlman plays *Fantasy on Carmen* by vibrating gut strings with rosin-rubbed horsehair fibers. Yachts are strung almost as tightly as his violin, tuned-up with stainless steel rigging cable; the sail-handling aboardship is done with Dacron line, and the anchor is connected to the bobbing boat with stretchy nylon.

Spin fishermen cast almost in-

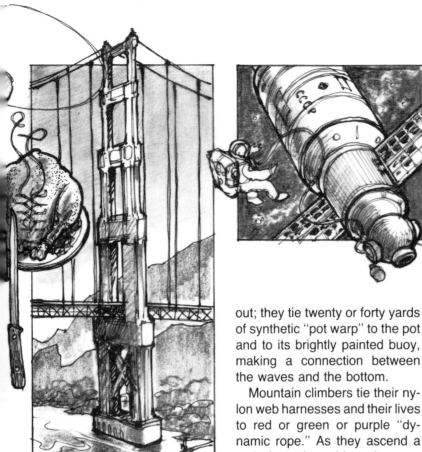

visible monofilament nylon to entice bass. Fly fishermen write S's of tip-weighted braided string in the air, hoping to drop an irresistible dry fly just over a huge trout. Cod fishermen tow nylon trawl nets the size of supermarket parking lots through the black Atlantic deeps. Lobstermen on their days ashore weave the Dacron head nets that let lobster into their baited pots . . . but not

out; they tie twenty or forty yards of synthetic "pot warp" to the pot and to its brightly painted buoy, making a connection between the waves and the bottom.

Mountain climbers tie their nylon web harnesses and their lives to red or green or purple "dynamic rope." As they ascend a rock face they drive pitons or force chocks into the rock cracks; they snap a spring-loaded carabiner into the holdfast and keep going up, leaving a trail of carabiners that guide and hold the rope. A loose rock, lost footing, and the mountaineer falls! But only past the last "beaner"; the rope catches and stretches to swing the climber back to the rock face.

Roofers haul up casks of nails and barrels of pitch on tarstained Manila lines. Cooks truss up stuffed turkeys with cotton

string. Clerks gift wrap boxes of truffles in ribbon. Workers in frame shops attach wire string behind paintings. Truckers lash tarpaulins over bulky loads with braided cord to keep them in place. Masons pull white cotton string tight and level to gauge the truth of their brick courses.

At sea, an aircraft carrier matches speeds with its tanker. A gun shoots a carefully coiled, light, heaving line from one to the other. The light line is used to snake a heavier line across. The heavier line brings a thick hawser, and the hawser hauls across a black refueling hose for a high-pressure fill-up. A Sea Stallion helicopter flies off the deck to rescue downed fliers; it hovers over them and lets down a welcome lifeline.

Parachutes float down on nylon webbing, about the same webbing that makes a good leash for your dog. Cords attach your sunglasses to your neck, your compass to your shirt, your racketball raquet to your wrist. Monofilament or gut crisscrosses a raquet for tennis or squash. A basketball swishes through a hoop and its cotton string net.

String. Clothes hanging from a clothesline and Cosmonaut Dzhanibekov hanging outside the Salyut space station on thin, light, storable, useful, multipurpose string.

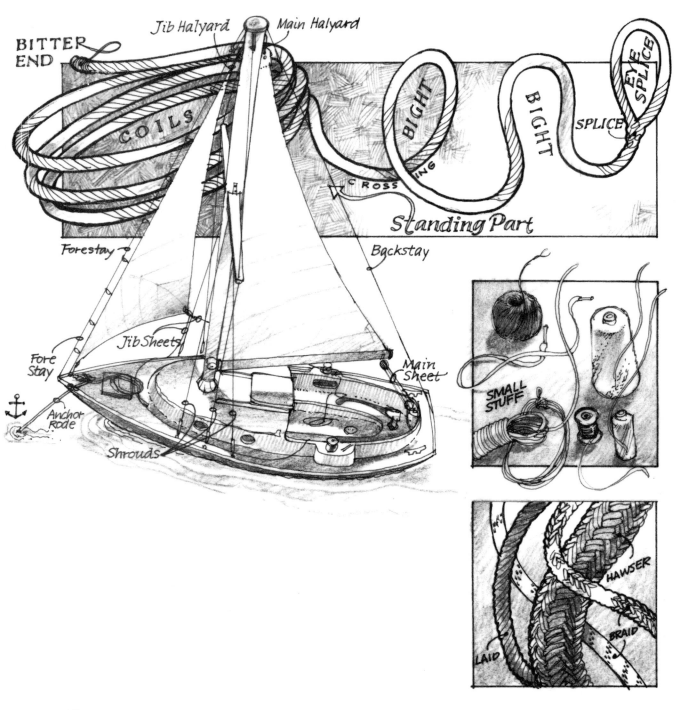

BITTER
END

Jib Halyard   Main Halyard

COILS

BIGHT   BIGHT   SPLICE   EYE SPLICE

CROSSING

Standing Part

Forestay   Backstay

Jib Sheets

Fore
Stay

Main
Sheet

Anchor
Rode

Shrouds

SMALL
STUFF

LAID   HAWSER   BRAID

Line Calls

Line has three parts, right? Two ends and the wiggly stuff in the middle.

Whoa! We'd better stop here and talk about *talking about* string. It's not as easy as talking about locomotives or vegetables, because one piece of rope looks very much like any other piece.

Some terms are general. *Cordage* is the whole ball of twine, every kind of string and line and rope and cable. *Line* is almost any kind of twisted, woven, or braided fiber, no matter what the size. *Small stuff* is light line, like cotton string or nylon cord or shoelaces or package twine or thread or *marline* (two- or three-strand twisted cord soaked in light tar. It smells wonderful).

Rope is a general term that refers to larger line—from about a quarter of an inch to two inches in diameter. The word *rope*, when used aboard a vessel, is always followed with nasty laughter; each kind of line on a vessel has its own specific name and sailors like to think that only feeble-minded people ashore call lines ropes. On board, a *sheet* controls a sail, while a *halyard* hoists it up. An anchor is attached to the boat with line or *rode*. Masts are supported fore-and-aft (forward and backward) by *stays*, athwart-ship (side to side) by *shrouds*. In recent years these both have been stainless steel *cables*. Flags and signals and center-boards are hoisted with *pendants*. Really thick line, over two inches in diameter, can be called *hawser*. It may sound fussy of sailors to have all these names for different lines, but they know how hard it is to shout good directions during a storm, and they

know that one line looks very much like another: wiggly stuff between two ends.

Laid line is twisted up, usually in three or four strands. *Braided line* is woven; it can be solid braid, hollow braid around a core of unwoven fibers, or braid around an inner braid.

A *coil* is line in orderly loops. If you are working toward the end of a line, the part that is tied down or trailing away is called the *standing part*. A small or large bend in a line is called a *bight*. A *crossing* is where one part of a line crosses another. The very end of the line you are dealing with is the *bitter end*, a usage both poetic and correct.

Line—laid or braided—can be woven back into itself or another line with a *splice*. If it forms a bight at the end, the loop is called an *eye splice*.

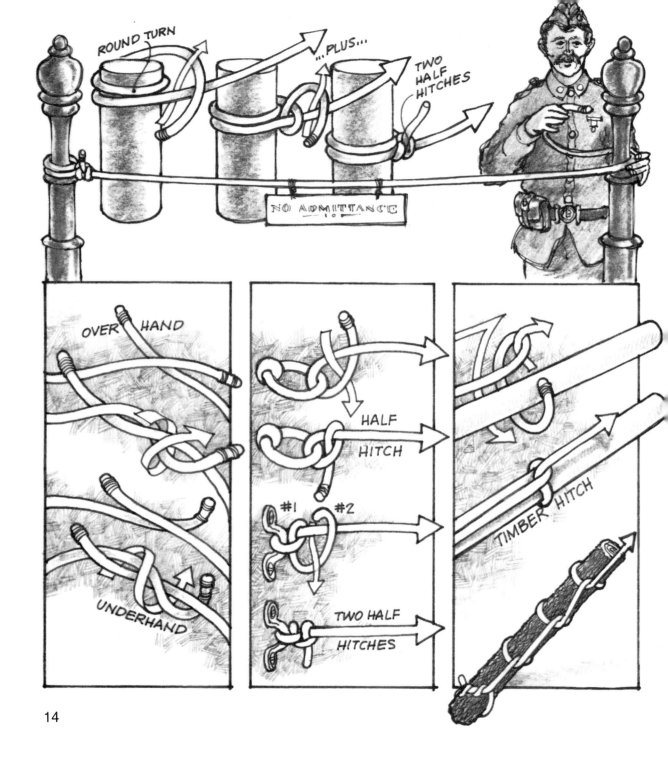

ROUND TURN

...PLUS...

TWO HALF HITCHES

NO ADMITTANCE

OVER HAND

UNDERHAND

HALF HITCH

#1 #2

TWO HALF HITCHES

TIMBER HITCH

If a line changes direction around an object or another piece of line, it makes a *turn*, but a *round turn* is more specific: A round turn makes at least a full circle and sometimes more. In Britain's Royal Navy young sailors are taught that "a Round Turn saved her majesty's ship," meaning that, like all knots, the round turn is a friction device that could allow one person to hold a heavy ship safely at the dock.

In an *overhand knot* the left line goes over and around the right line. In an *underhand knot* the left goes under and around the right.

To make a *half hitch*, the end of the line makes a round turn (about an object or another piece of line) and then leads through the turn. The simplest (and sometimes best) way to *hitch* (attach) a line to an object is a round turn and two half hitches around the standing part of the line.

The *timber hitch* makes a round turn at a right angle to the standing part and leads under itself. You can see that as the strain on the line is heavier, it will squeeze tighter.

Whipping

A *whipping* is a binding that prevents the bitter end from falling apart. Since you can't do good work with a line-end that looks like a parsley sprig, every line needs to be whipped, a small investment in time that repays you in later convenience. Synthetic small stuff and light line up to about three-sixteenths of an inch respond well to searing with a match or lighter.

For larger line the *sailor's whipping* made with a needle and sail twine is the most lasting and practical. Starting with an anchor knot in one strand or through a braided line's diameter, the turns are made toward the end, tight enough to constrict and stiffen the line. At the head of the wrapping (which should be about one-third longer than the diameter of the line) the needle passes through one strand—or about a third of a braided line. In laid line (with strands), the needle and twine emerge in the cleft between strands and follow the line of cleft across the wrappings, where they pass through another strand. Passing through three strands and following three clefts, the whipping is finished with one or two half-hitches tucked into a cleft.

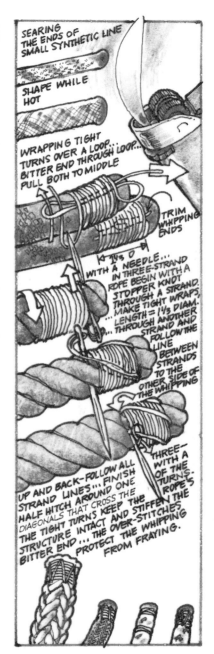

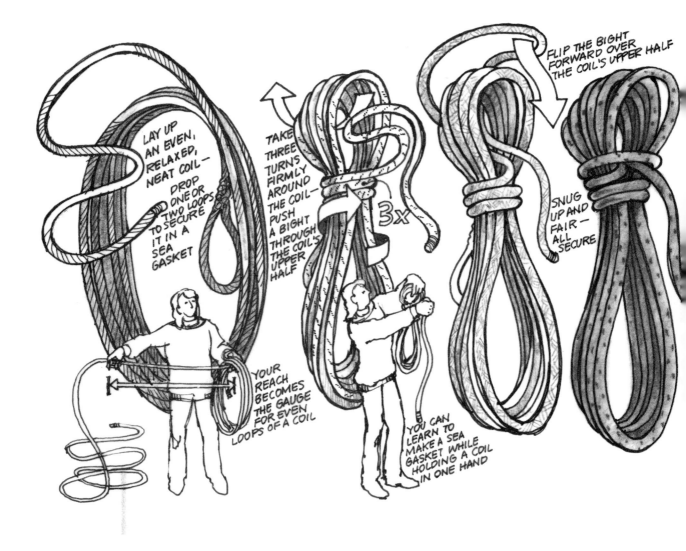

LAY UP AN EVEN, RELAXED, NEAT COIL—DROP ONE OR TWO LOOPS TO SECURE IT IN A SEA GASKET

YOUR REACH BECOMES THE GAUGE FOR EVEN LOOPS OF A COIL

TAKE THREE TURNS FIRMLY AROUND THE COIL— PUSH A BIGHT THROUGH THE COIL'S UPPER HALF

3x

YOU CAN LEARN TO MAKE A SEA GASKET WHILE HOLDING A COIL IN ONE HAND

FLIP THE BIGHT FORWARD OVER THE COIL'S UPPER HALF

SNUG UP AND FAIR—ALL SECURE

Drop a Line to Show You Care

What is useful? A flashlight is a gladsome thing on a dark, stormy night. Not so much the flashlight as its light; a dead flashlight will not cut the gloom of a garage as something scratches and breathes noisily in the corner.

Line is useful only if you can turn it on. It must be ready. If your boat is docking and you give a yachtswoman a shopping bag full of tangled dock line, she will not thank you. A businesslike coil of dry, clean line brings out her best effort.

String wants to be stored well. Bits of braid for tying down the odd watermelon want small,

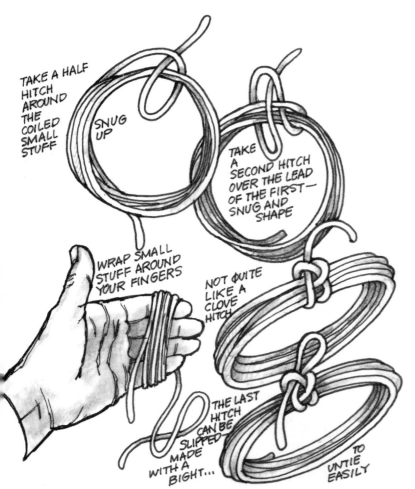

TAKE A HALF HITCH AROUND THE COILED SMALL STUFF

SNUG UP

TAKE A SECOND HITCH OVER THE LEAD OF THE FIRST— SNUG AND SHAPE

WRAP SMALL STUFF AROUND YOUR FINGERS

NOT QUITE LIKE A CLOVE HITCH

THE LAST HITCH CAN BE SLIPPED MADE WITH A BIGHT...

TO UNTIE EASILY

TO SECURE A COIL TO A MAST—
1. REACH THROUGH THE COIL TO PULL OUT A BIGHT—
2. TWIST IT TWO OR THREE TIMES CLOCKWISE—
3. TAKE A ROUND TURN ABOUT THE COILED LINE WITH THE BIGHT
4. PUT THE TWISTED LOOP END OVER THE HORN OF THE CLEAT

FIGURE EIGHTS

"FLAKE" DOWN WET ROPE TO DRY IN SHADE AND IN OVERLAPPING FIGURE EIGHTS

snug coils. Lengths of line ready to lash two-by-fours to your car rack want longer, looser, secure coils. Three hundred feet of anchor rode may be more useful in two or three coils.

Coils in large line should be big enough to allow circulation of air, to discourage mildew. They should be hung away from the sun to avoid damage from ultraviolet rays. Wet line—especially natural fiber lines—should be *flaked down* to dry thoroughly.

A *sea gasket* is a neat, secure coil that will not be knocked into piles of eel sculpture when a shovel is thrown in beside it.

17

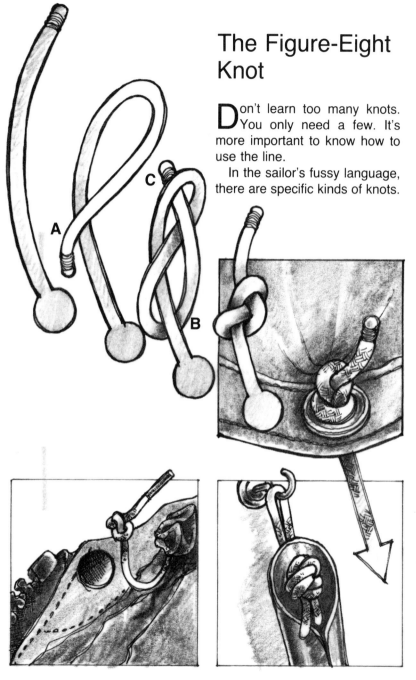

The Figure-Eight Knot

Don't learn too many knots. You only need a few. It's more important to know how to use the line.

In the sailor's fussy language, there are specific kinds of knots.

Most correctly, a *knot* is a knob, made in line to stop the line at a hole. A *hitch* attaches a line to an object. A *binding knot* closes around an object. A *bend* attaches one line to another line. There are also *loops* (which are usually temporary, like a bowline), *eyes* (usually permanent), and *nooses* (which are made to tighten up, like a *hangman's noose* or the lasso's *honda knot*).

The *figure-eight knot* is simple and useful. The bitter end moves around clockwise to make a loop. It crosses over the standing part [**A**] and passes under it to the right [**B**]. The bitter end then crosses over the downward leg of the original loop and goes through it [**C**].

The last step is the most important: The knot is tightened gradually and fingered into shape, or *faired*. Fairing is as important as tying.

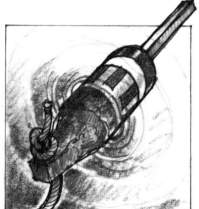

The Clove Hitch

A good knot has four virtues: It is easy to tie, it is stable (under load and through jerks), it reduces the strength of the line only a little, and it is easy to untie.

Knots are friction devices. The friction of turns and angles within a knot keeps it stable. Some knots use friction more efficiently than others, but every knot reduces the strength of the line it's tied in, as much as 60 percent for a poor knot.

The *clove hitch* is easy to tie but has limitations. It is begun with a round turn to the right [**A**]. The bitter end crosses over its own standing part and makes another round turn to the left [**B**]. Now the end runs under the second round turn [**C**]. Finally, the hitch is tightened and faired.

Using the clove hitch on dock pilings, the dock line is grasped from beneath with your thumb out to the right [**D**]. Turning your hand inward, you make a loop, which you drop over the piling [**E**]. Thumb to the right, repeat [**F**], tighten, and fair.

It is so quick to tie that you will use it to hang everything from coils of line to bag drawstrings. But use it with this caution: It is so simple that it can loosen with repeated jerking.

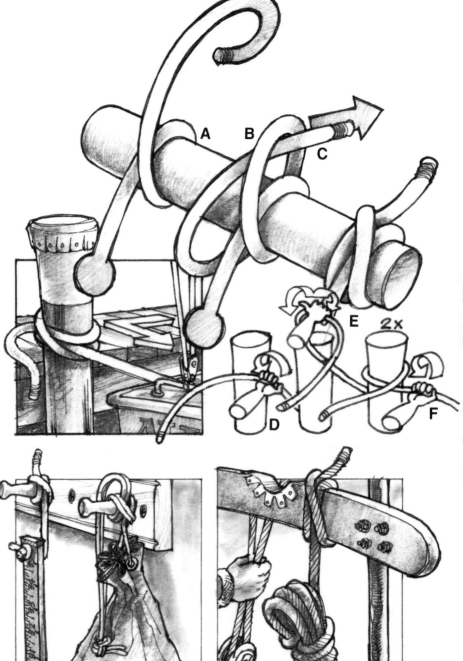

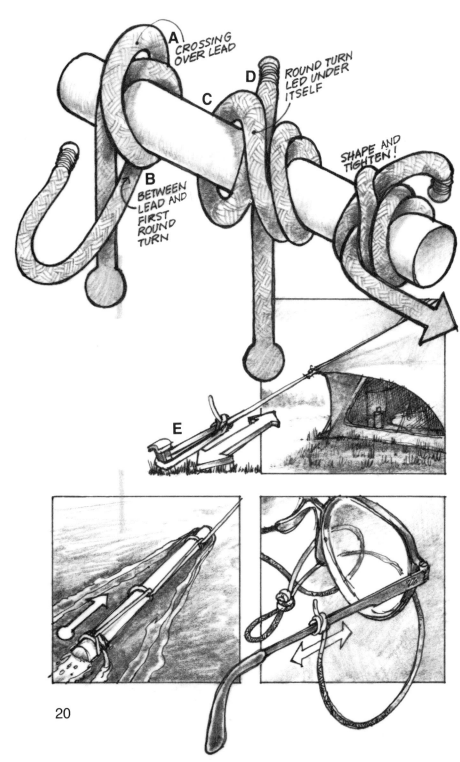

A CROSSING OVER LEAD

D ROUND TURN LED UNDER ITSELF

C

B BETWEEN LEAD AND FIRST ROUND TURN

SHAPE AND TIGHTEN!

E

The Rolling Hitch

The rolling hitch requires more care in tying but is more stable than a clove hitch. It is especially useful in *lengthwise pull* along a cylinder, plank, or even along a line.

It is begun with a round turn that crosses its own standing part to the left [**A**]. The bitter end returns to the right of the standing part and leads between the standing part and the round turn [**B**]. The end makes another round turn across the standing part to the left [**C**]. The bitter end is passed under this last round turn to the left of the standing part [**D**], and the hitch is snugged and faired.

This hitch is not symmetrical: It has two turns on one side of the standing part and a single turn on the other side. It can be tied to the right or to the left, but to resist lengthwise pull the two turns should be on the side toward the pull.

The rolling hitch can be used to adjust tent *guys* (yet another name for line). The guy makes a turn around the stake [**E**] and the rolling hitch fastens it to its own standing part. The two turns, in this case, are made on the tent-stake side, which is the direction of pull.

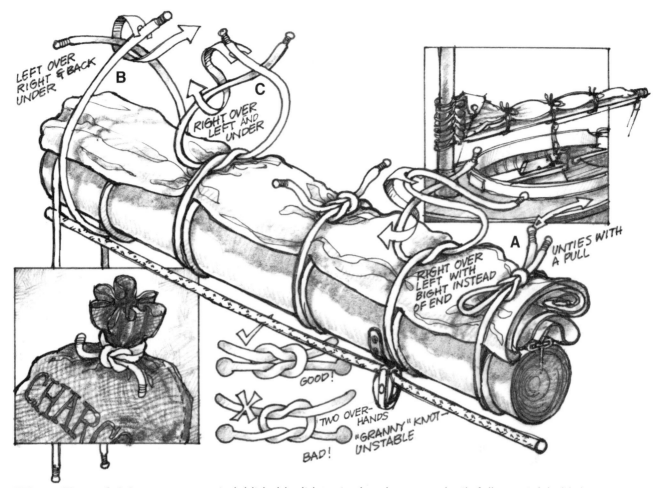

LEFT OVER RIGHT & BACK UNDER

B

RIGHT OVER LEFT AND UNDER

C

A

UNTIES WITH A PULL

RIGHT OVER LEFT WITH BIGHT INSTEAD OF END

CHARC

GOOD!

TWO OVER-HANDS

"GRANNY" KNOT— UNSTABLE

BAD!

The Reef Knot

The reef knot is a dangerous knot.

The reef knot is also called the *square knot* because of its pleasing pattern. It is a binding knot, well suited to gathering and holding. But . . . *it is only stable when it is supported against the ma-terial it holds*. It is not a bend—it is not designed to attach two lines in space and will *spill* (change its form and fail) if it is used as a bend.

It is used in three celebrated ways. On the water, it *reefs* sails (gathers them up to reduce sail area in high winds). For this, it is often *slipped*—tied with a bight instead of the bitter end [**A**]; when the end is pulled, the knot con-veniently falls apart. It holds bags and packages closed. When tied incorrectly it is so easy to undo that it is used on grain sacks and called a *granary knot* or *granny knot*. *Double slipped* (with two bights) it is a shoelace knot. (See copyright page.)

Tying it, the left end goes over and around the right [**B**]. The new right now goes over and around the left [**C**]. Snug and shape.

21

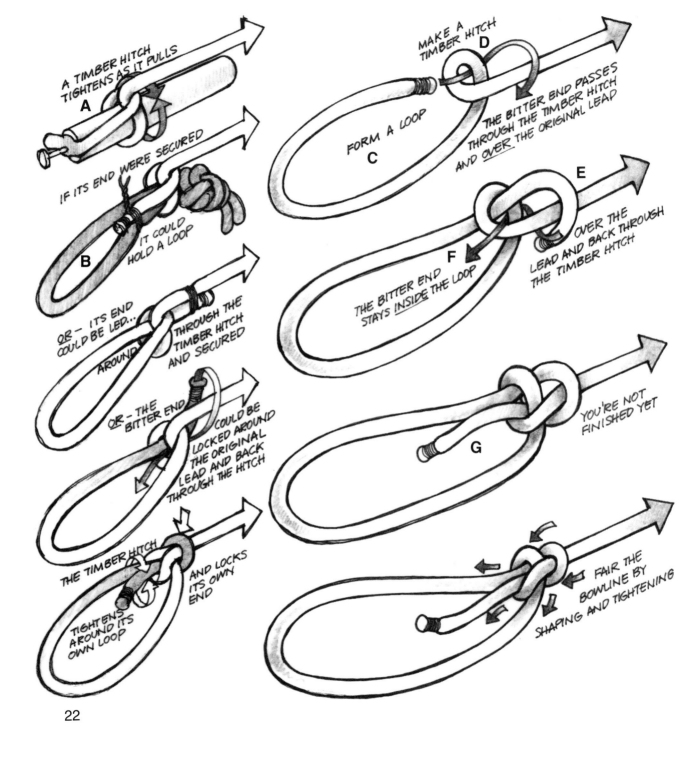

A TIMBER HITCH TIGHTENS AS IT PULLS

A

IF ITS END WERE SECURED

IT COULD HOLD A LOOP

B

OR — ITS END COULD BE LED...

AROUND

THROUGH THE TIMBER HITCH AND SECURED

OR — THE BITTER END COULD BE LOCKED AROUND THE ORIGINAL LEAD AND BACK THROUGH THE HITCH

THE TIMBER HITCH

AND LOCKS ITS OWN END

TIGHTENS AROUND ITS OWN LOOP

MAKE A TIMBER HITCH

D

FORM A LOOP

C

THE BITTER END PASSES THROUGH THE TIMBER HITCH AND <u>OVER</u> THE ORIGINAL LEAD

E

OVER THE LEAD AND BACK THROUGH THE TIMBER HITCH

THE BITTER END STAYS <u>INSIDE</u> THE LOOP

F

YOU'RE NOT FINISHED YET

G

FAIR THE BOWLINE BY SHAPING AND TIGHTENING

The Bowline

The Abraham Lincoln of knots—common, useful, strong, deceptively subtle, and elegant in its simplicity—the *bowline* is used everywhere a loop is needed. Knowing how to use the bowline makes the difference between messing with string and using it.

There are a dozen clever ways to tie the bowline. Forget about rabbits coming out of holes and trick ties and learn the bowline's structure. Then you can tie it upside down, backward, and crossways and still know you've done it right.

The bowline uses a timber hitch [**A**] to secure a loop [**B**]. A bight is formed [**C**], and the bight's bitter end is led through a timber hitch [**D**]. The end makes a turn around the standing part [**E**] and returns through the timber hitch [**F**]. The bitter end stays *inside* the loop [**G**], where it is less likely to hang up on something. Once the bowline is snugged and faired, it is ready for use.

The bowline has all the virtues: It is easy to tie, it is secure, it retains over 70 percent of the line's strength, and it is easy to untie even after it has held a heavy load.

Before it unties, the bowline unlocks, using the "handle" around the standing part [**H**] as a key. When the standing part is relaxed, the handle folds down [**I**] and the bowline will yield.

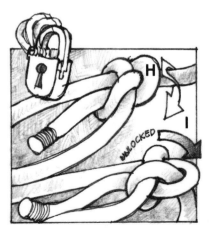

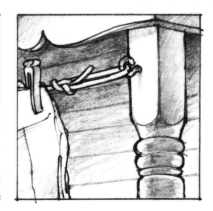

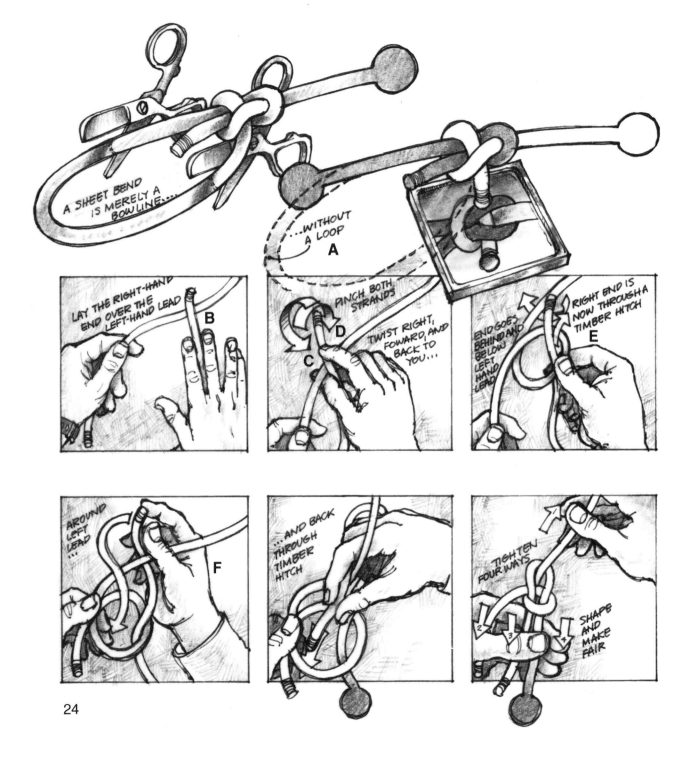

A SHEET BEND IS MERELY A _BOWLINE_....

...WITHOUT A LOOP

A

LAY THE RIGHT-HAND END OVER THE LEFT-HAND LEAD

B

PINCH BOTH STRANDS

TWIST RIGHT, FOWARD, AND BACK TO YOU...

C **D**

END GOES BEHIND AND BELOW LEFT HAND LEAD

RIGHT END IS NOW THROUGH A TIMBER HITCH

E

AROUND LEFT LEAD...

F

...AND BACK THROUGH TIMBER HITCH

TIGHTEN FOUR WAYS

SHAPE AND MAKE FAIR

The Sheet Bend

In a sensible world there would be no need to join one line and another: The first line would always be long enough. The question should always rise in your mind when you are bending lines: "Should I use a longer line?" Even a fine knot like the *sheet bend* concentrates the strain of pull in itself, reduces the strength of the line, and gets caught in the smallest obstacle with what has been called "the malevolent intelligence of line."

This is the real world, though, and the sheet bend is the easiest and simplest tool for the job. It has all the virtues of the bowline because it *is* a bowline . . . without the loop [**A**]. It is tied exactly like the bowline and unties as smartly.

Knowing a knot's structure and building it is the best way to tie a knot. But here is one of the "quick" methods. Lay one line over another [**B**], grasp both between finger and thumb [**C**], fold forward and under [**D**]. When the bitter end returns from its little trip it is within a round turn [**E**]. Take it behind the standing part and back through the turn [**F**], snug and fair.

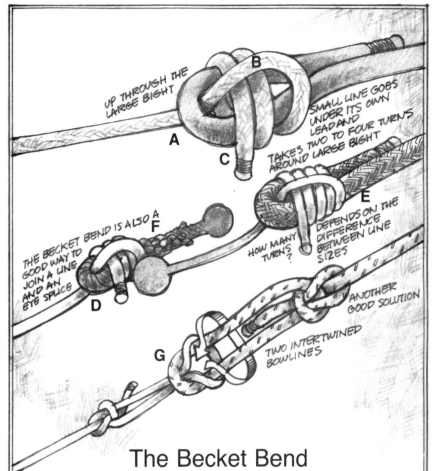

UP THROUGH THE LARGE BIGHT

SMALL LINE GOES UNDER ITS OWN LEAD AND TAKES TWO TO FOUR TURNS AROUND LARGE BIGHT

THE BECKET BEND IS ALSO A GOOD WAY TO JOIN A LINE AND AN EYE SPLICE

HOW MANY TURNS?

DEPENDS ON THE DIFFERENCE BETWEEN LINE SIZES

ANOTHER GOOD SOLUTION

TWO INTERTWINED BOWLINES

The Becket Bend

The *becket bend* is a secure way to bend a small line to a larger line, but it requires careful forming and fairing. A bight is formed in the larger line [**A**] and the end of the smaller line leads up through it [**B**]. Several turns are taken around both legs of the larger line's bight, under the light line's lead [**C**]. The number of turns varies from two or three for lines of slightly differing diameter [**D**], to half a dozen for lines of dissimilar size [**E**].

The becket bend is workable for eye splices, too [**F**].

One of the most secure bends for dissimilar lines is an arrangement of bowlines intertwined to form a reef knot in two bights [**G**].

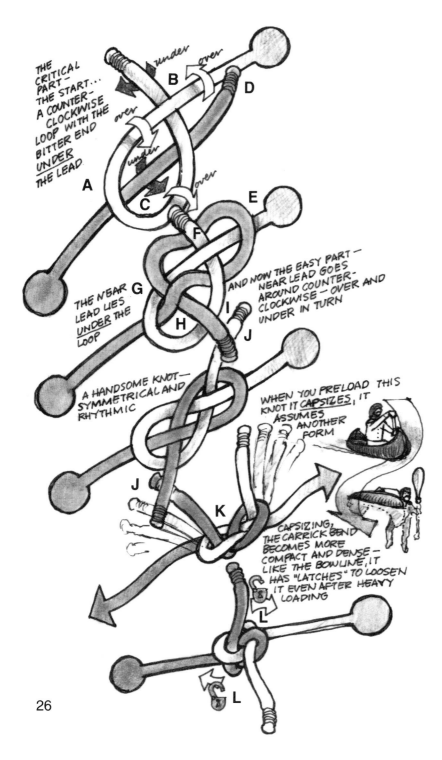

THE CRITICAL PART — THE START... A COUNTER-CLOCKWISE LOOP WITH THE BITTER END **UNDER THE LEAD**

under over

B **D**

over

under

A

over

C

E

F

THE NEAR LEAD LIES **UNDER THE** LOOP

G

AND NOW THE EASY PART — NEAR LEAD GOES AROUND COUNTER-CLOCKWISE — OVER AND UNDER IN TURN

I

H

J

A HANDSOME KNOT — SYMMETRICAL AND RHYTHMIC

WHEN YOU PRELOAD THIS KNOT IT **CAPSIZES**, IT ASSUMES ANOTHER FORM

J

K

CAPSIZING, THE CARRICK BEND BECOMES MORE COMPACT AND DENSE — LIKE THE BOWLINE, IT HAS "LATCHES" TO LOOSEN IT EVEN AFTER HEAVY LOADING

L

L

26

The Carrick Bend

Like a water buffalo, the *carrick bend* is strong, dependable, and difficult to handle. For absolute security under heavy loads, it is a wise choice, but tying it requires skill and practice.

Start with a bight made counterclockwise [**A**], passing the bitter end under the standing part [**B**]. Bring the second line under the open loop of the first [**C**] and travel counterclockwise, over-under, around the knot [**D**], over the upper standing part [**E**], under the upper bitter end [**F**], over one leg of the upper loop [**G**], under the standing part of the lower line [**H**], and over the remaining leg of the upper loop [**I**].

This interlocking weave creates a symmetrical, almost decorative knot that performs a surprising trick. Leave the bitter ends of both lines long [**J, J**], because loading causes the carrick bend to *capsize* into a more compact and stable form [**K**].

This knot has two "latches," or handles, that unlock it [**L, L**].

Hunter's Bend

Inventing a knot at this late date seems unlikely. There are only so many ways to cook eggs. But in 1978 Dr. Edward Hunter devised a new knot to connect slippery synthetic lines. Called *Hunter's bend*, it is easy to tie, and it is secure, strong, and holds the line well. Like the carrick bend, it unties with two handles.

Hunter's bend is a demanding knot. It takes practice to plant it firmly in your mind. Once planted it can take root and grow into a tool.

The lines to be joined are laid parallel with the standing part from the right, in front [**A**]. Keeping the lines neat and parallel, a counterclockwise loop is made; the ends will be inside the standing parts [**B, B**]. The bitter end from one side of the loop crosses under the loop and passes through from the opposite side; the bitter end from the other side of the loop does the same [**C, C**]. The standing parts are pulled to capsize the bend into its new form [**D**]: on one side, two handles and two parallel turns [**E**], on the other side, two diagonal turns [**F**].

I wish I'd thought of it before Dr. Hunter.

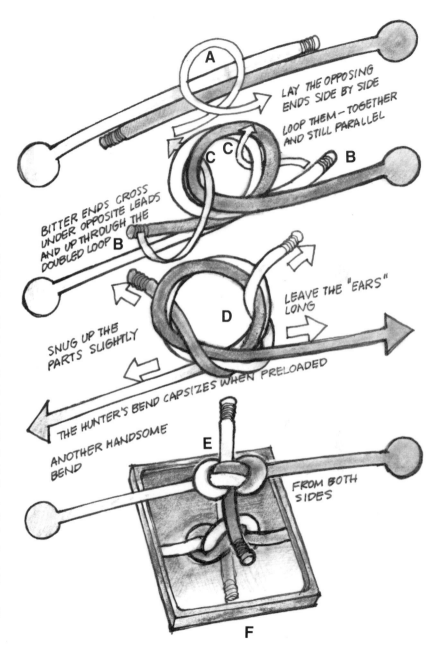

LAY THE OPPOSING ENDS SIDE BY SIDE

LOOP THEM — TOGETHER AND STILL PARALLEL

BITTER ENDS CROSS UNDER OPPOSITE LEADS AND UP THROUGH THE DOUBLED LOOP

LEAVE THE "EARS" LONG

SNUG UP THE PARTS SLIGHTLY

THE HUNTER'S BEND CAPSIZES WHEN PRELOADED

ANOTHER HANDSOME BEND

FROM BOTH SIDES

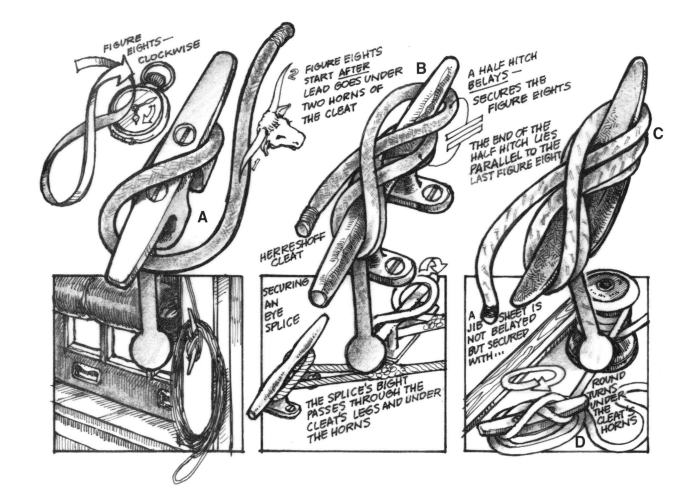

FIGURE EIGHTS—CLOCKWISE

2 FIGURE EIGHTS START AFTER LEAD GOES UNDER TWO HORNS OF THE CLEAT

A

HERRESHOFF CLEAT

SECURING AN EYE SPLICE

THE SPLICE'S BIGHT PASSES THROUGH THE CLEATS LEGS AND UNDER THE HORNS

B

A HALF HITCH BELAYS—SECURES THE FIGURE EIGHTS

THE END OF THE HALF HITCH LIES PARALLEL TO THE LAST FIGURE EIGHT

C

A JIB SHEET IS NOT BELAYED BUT SECURED WITH...

ROUND TURNS UNDER THE CLEAT'S HORNS

D

Cleating

Friction gives you control.

The friction in a knot holds line. The friction around a *cleat* allows you to control line, to let out or bring in the length of line beyond the cleat.

The standing part of a line leads under *both* horns of a cleat [**A**] and into figure-eight turns that build up the friction. With this simple tool, about as complicated as a shovel, a small person can hold and safely release a controlled amount of line to an enormous sail or a boat straining at the dock. When the right amount of line is played out, the line can be cleated and *belayed* or *made fast*—locked: After two or three figure-eights, a half hitch is folded under and snugged around one horn [**B**]. The end of

A HALYARD LEADS UNDER THE PIN THEN FIGURE EIGHTS ENDING WITH A HALF HITCH

A FIFE RAIL WITH BELAYING PINS

E

F

G

HALF HITCH

H

START WITH A ROUND TURN

I

HEAVY HAWSER

END WITH HALF HITCHES

the hitch should lie parallel to the last figure-eight [**C**].

Because things happen quickly on a small boat, the sheets (lines that control sails) on a small boat are most often secured with a quick-on, quick-off wrap or two around the base of the cleat [**D**].

An eye splice can be made fast to a cleat by passing its loop through the cleat's legs and folding it over both horns.

In older boats, lines aloft were often controlled with *belaying pins*. The standing part was led under and around the pin's leg [**E**], the line was adjusted, then secured with figure-eights between the foot and head of the pin [**F**], and finished with a half hitch around the head [**G**].

Anchor rode or docking lines can be controlled from a *samson post* on the foredeck [**H**]. Two control turns are taken around the post before figure-eights and a half hitch on the horizontal pin secure the line.

Twin *bollards* (posts) [**I**] control heavy lines with figure-eights. Two half hitches around the standing part belay the line.

Yesterday's news can be stacked as businesslike bundles with stout twine. Make a noose by feeding the standing end of a small bowline through its loop. Snare the bundle and pull against the bowline [**A**], using it like a crude pulley. This gives you a mechanical advantage; don't break the twine. Lead the twine at a right angle to the first loop around the bundle and make a *crossing knot* [**B**] to secure the intersection of lines. Pass the line under and around the bowline and pull against it (more advantage) [**C**]. Take the bitter end under the bowline again and secure with two half hitches on the far side.

Binding a Bundle

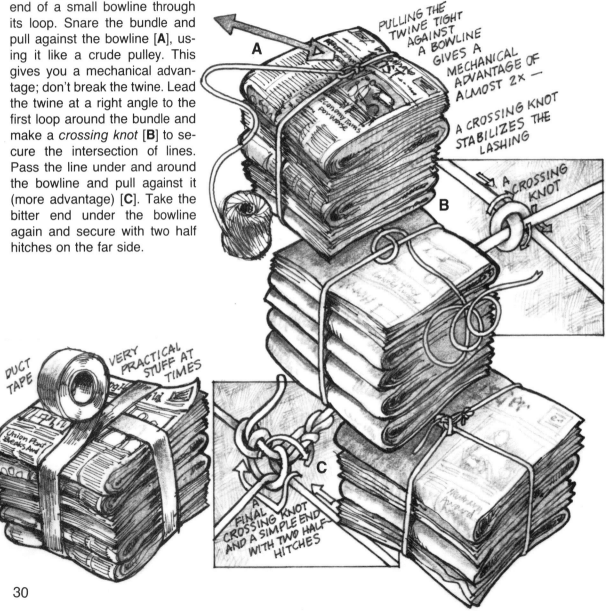

PULLING THE TWINE TIGHT AGAINST A BOWLINE GIVES A MECHANICAL ADVANTAGE OF ALMOST 2x —

A CROSSING KNOT STABILIZES THE LASHING

A CROSSING KNOT

DUCT TAPE

VERY PRACTICAL STUFF AT TIMES

A FINAL CROSSING KNOT AND A SIMPLE END WITH TWO HALF HITCHES

30

Bows

Hundreds of *bows* for satin and grosgrain ribbon are lost to us; most ribbons today are machine tied and blister packaged. Here are two holdovers. Take several neat turns of ribbon [**A**] and fold them in half. Make a narrow waist by snipping away the inside corners of the turns [**B**]. Wrap your gift with ribbon and secure with a reef knot, leaving long ends [**C**]. Tie another reef knot across the unfolded narrowing at the waist [**D**]. Fan and fluff out the turns in the fold to make a bow [**E**].

You can also make a spiral of several turns and secure it with a reef knot [**F**].

SEVERAL TURNS OF RIBBON

A

FLATTENED

FOLDED IN HALF

THE INSIDE CORNERS SNIPPED...

B

LAID FULL ACROSS THE RIBBON LASHING

A SIMPLE SPIRAL OF RIBBON BOUND TO THE LASHINGS AS A FALSE BOW

F

AND FASTENED WITH A REEF KNOT

C

D

THE INNER TURNS ARE PULLED OUT IN SEQUENCE TO MAKE A DECORATIVE BOW

E

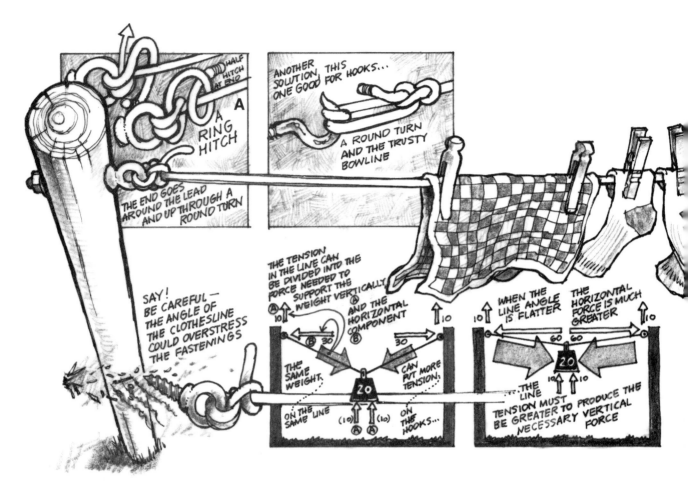

Rigging a Clothesline

A domestic schooner with a full press of household sail, the clothesline is a monument to appropriate technology.

Begin at the far end with a *ring hitch* [**A**], designed to attach an anchor's rode to its shackle or a hoisting line to a bucket's bail. Af-ter taking a round turn, lead the end around the standing part and through the turn. Secure with a half hitch, snug, and fair.

To adjust the tension of the line at the porch end, use a *trucker's comealong* [**B**]. This simple line tool multiplies your strength when tightening a line across a yard or across the load on a trailer truck. Make a loop about two feet from the porch; you can use a figure-eight in the bight [**C**], or a bight pushed through a tim-ber hitch [**D**]. Lead the end through a hook or eyebolt on the

C

D

A FIGURE-EIGHT NOOSE

AND A

E

ROLLING HITCH

TIMBER HITCH WITH A BIGHT THRUST THROUGH IT

THE NOOSE AND RING WORK LIKE CRUDE BLOCKS

MECH. ADV. ≅ 2×

B

RING HITCH

porch and back through the loop. Pull against the loop, and secure it with a rolling hitch [**E**] across both parts of the line.

A tight clothesline makes for a businesslike yard, but before you hang a wet rug on it, remember that you are hanging a vertical weight from a horizontal line. You are working with two separate forces: *out* and *up*. If a clothesline were hanging at a forty-five degree angle, the *out* and *up* forces would be about equal. But at a shallow angle, the *out* forces must increase enormously to provide a little *up* force. If you had a steel cable clothesline and strong fasteners, you could swing on the clothesline and pull the porch down. Line not only has a malevolent intelligence but backs it up with dangerous strength.

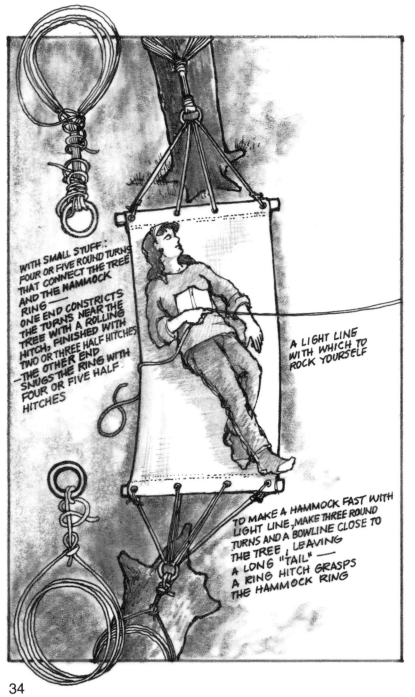

WITH SMALL STUFF: FOUR OR FIVE ROUND TURNS THAT CONNECT THE TREE AND THE HAMMOCK RING —
ONE END CONSTRICTS THE TURNS NEAR THE TREE WITH A ROLLING HITCH, FINISHED WITH TWO OR THREE HALF HITCHES — THE OTHER END SNUGS THE RING WITH FOUR OR FIVE HALF HITCHES

A LIGHT LINE WITH WHICH TO ROCK YOURSELF

TO MAKE A HAMMOCK FAST WITH LIGHT LINE, MAKE THREE ROUND TURNS AND A BOWLINE CLOSE TO THE TREE, LEAVING A LONG "TAIL" — A RING HITCH GRASPS THE HAMMOCK RING

Swinging a Hammock

Sudden hammock failure has caused the death of many daydreams. Remember the angles and the forces involved when you are rigging a hammock. You will need more than a cup hook in a two-by-four or a wispy sapling to hold it up.

A single line can "walk" down a tree trunk. You could use several turns of small, strong cord around the trunk and through the hammock's ring, tightening the cords at the ring and near the trunk with rolling hitches. You could also make several turns of larger line around the trunk and tie a bowline close to the tree.

Swigging is a way of using the multiplying effect of angles to your advantage in tugging up a sail or pulling up a load. The vertical line is pulled horizontally, increasing the force along the line. The swigger pulls out, and in the same motion brings the slack gained down toward a cleat with his body weight, where a shipmate takes it up across turns on a cleat.

Another way of multiplying strength is to harness gullible friends, using the *artilleryman's loop.*

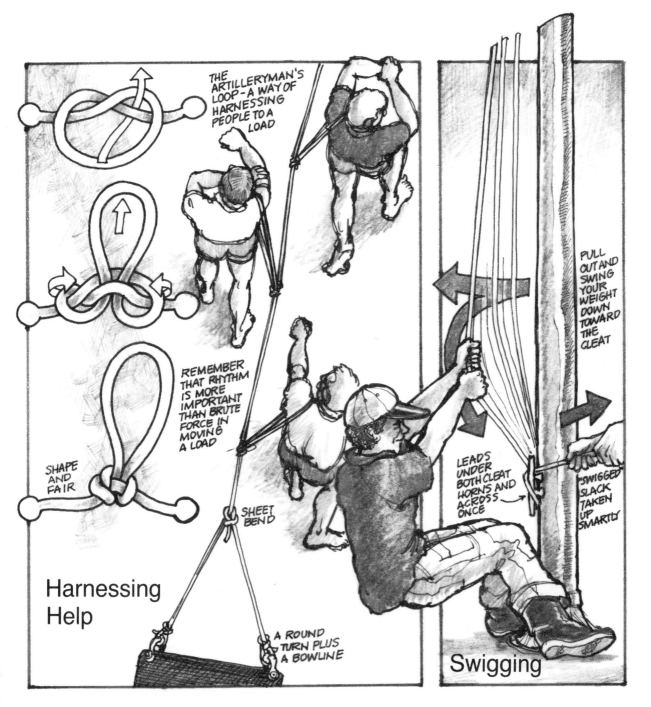

THE ARTILLERYMAN'S LOOP – A WAY OF HARNESSING PEOPLE TO A LOAD

SHAPE AND FAIR

REMEMBER THAT RHYTHM IS MORE IMPORTANT THAN BRUTE FORCE IN MOVING A LOAD

SHEET BEND

A ROUND TURN PLUS A BOWLINE

PULL OUT AND SWING YOUR WEIGHT DOWN TOWARD THE CLEAT

LEADS UNDER BOTH CLEAT HORNS AND ACROSS ONCE

"SWIGGED" SLACK TAKEN UP SMARTLY

Harnessing Help

Swigging

Hauling

Big loads, little cars, common problem. Lashing any load is a little exercise in engineering, counteracting three forces: side-to-side, forward-and-back, up-and-down.

When you haul a canoe, most of the forward-and-back and the up-and-down strains are taken by the bow and stern lines. From a bowline [**A**], lead the lines down across smooth or padded edges to solid points on the bumper or under the car [**B**]. A hardware store S-hook is a useful tool [**C**]. Pass the end through the bowline and pull down against it [**D**]; this gives you a mechanical advantage. Secure with a rolling hitch around the two diverging lines [**E**] (forcing them together gives you more advantage).

The sideways strains will be taken by the cartop carrier. Start with a simple bowline around one beam [**F**]. Cross the canoe and tighten, keeping the tension with a round turn on the far beam's end [**G**]. Make two side-to-side and two diagonal passes, an-

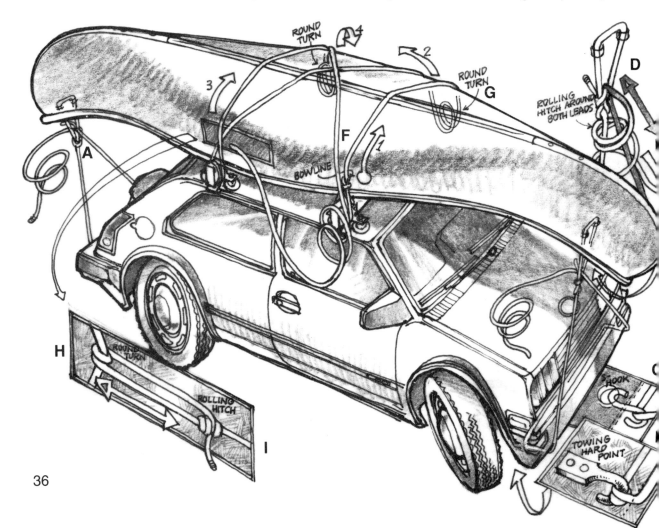

choring with a round turn each time. Tighten the whole system at the end by catching one of the diagonals with a round turn and pulling it sideways (a mechanical advantage) [H], then securing with a rolling hitch [I].

Hauling four-by-eight sheets of plywood is never easy. Rooftop pads protect your roof and give more bearing surface [J]. Start with a bowline around a solid point at the rear bumper [K] and go forward diagonally with enough tension to bend down the plywood. Lead across the front [L] and back toward the rear [M], pulling down and securing. The plywood should curve downward. Tying the plywood side to side, remember that a shallow angle in to a roof rack or even through the windows and under the car roof is not good; a line at that angle cannot exert good downward force. Take a line from a point *under* the car and lead it over the plywood. Use a trucker's comealong to tighten up. Add another downlashing at the rear [N]. Drive slowly. Good luck.

When lashing bags on to a cartop rack, secure the tension in each part of the line by taking round turns, and remember to think of all three directions.

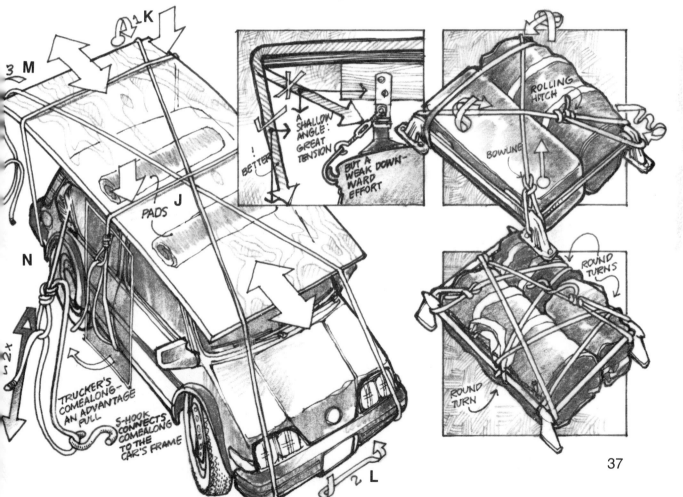

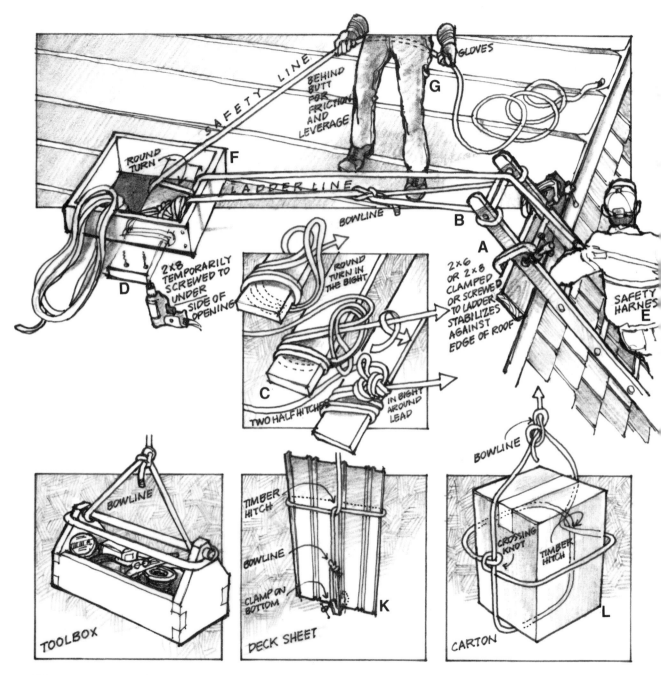

SAFETY LINE

BEHIND BUTT FOR FRICTION AND LEVERAGE

GLOVES

G

ROUND TURN

F

LADDER LINE

BOWLINE

B

A

2×8 TEMPORARILY SCREWED TO UNDER SIDE OF OPENING

D

2×6 OR 2×8 CLAMPED OR SCREWED TO LADDER STABILIZES AGAINST EDGE OF ROOF

SAFETY HARNESS

E

ROUND TURN IN THE BIGHT

IN BIGHT AROUND LEAD

C

TWO HALF HITCHES

BOWLINE

TOOLBOX

TIMBER HITCH

BOWLINE

CLAMP ON BOTTOM

K

DECK SHEET

BOWLINE

CROSSING KNOT

TIMBER HITCH

L

CARTON

38

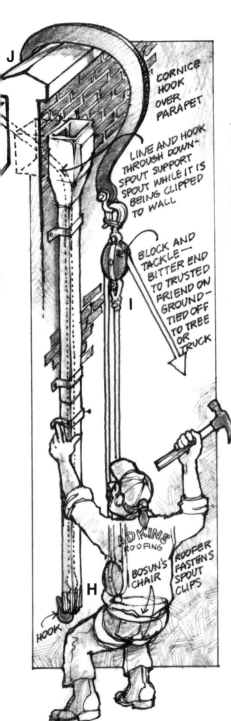

On the Roof

It's a long way down. Even twenty feet is too far to fall. But the view from a roof can be lovely.

Be especially careful working up high. Keep your ladder secure with blocks [A] and a safety line [B] tied off [C] to a solid beam or a temporarily screwed-in plank [D]. Wear a safety harness or, at least, a bowline under your arms [E]. Either should be hitched to a safety line that makes a round turn about a solid plank [F] and goes to a trusted friend, who holds the line—with gloves—under his bottom [G]. Mountain climbers call this arrangement *on belay*, and you shouldn't go higher than a grandfather clock without it.

Roofers have their tricks to work heights . . . bosun's chairs [H], blocks and tackles [I], cornice hooks [J], and others. A lot of their work involves hoisting tools and materials up to the roof. My father and grandfather were roofers and I have always admired their grace up high and their cleverness with rigging line. Rigging a sheet of steel deck [K] or a boxed fan [L] to be hoisted requires thought and care. Even preparing a hammer or a toolbox for the trip requires a small piece of line engineering.

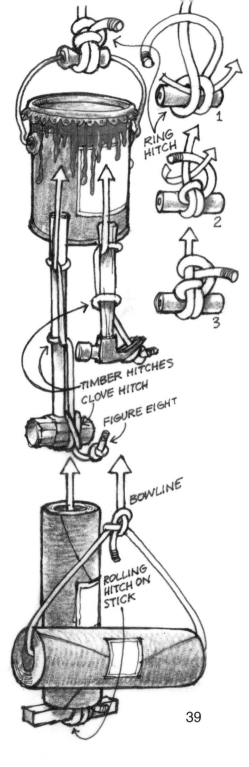

39

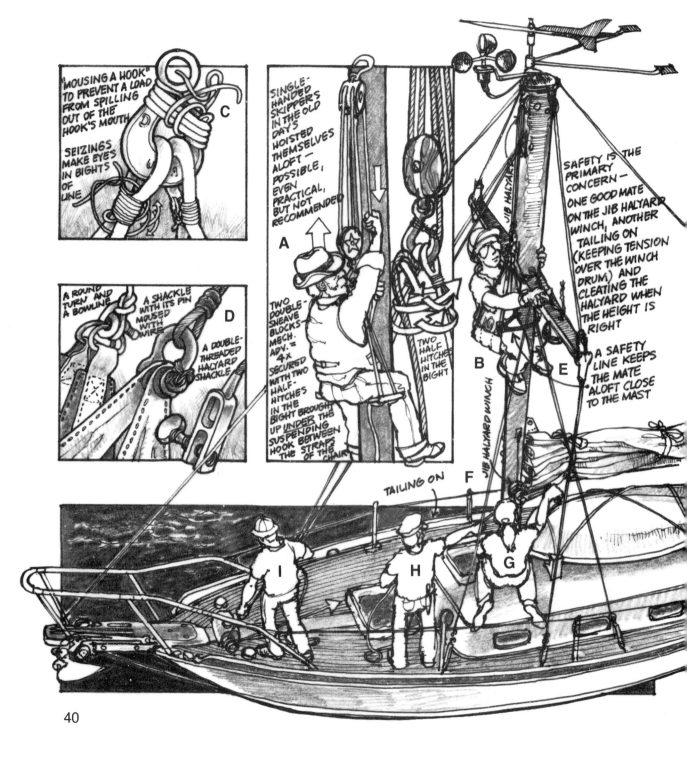

C — "MOUSING A HOOK" TO PREVENT A LOAD FROM SPILLING OUT OF THE HOOK'S MOUTH

SEIZINGS MAKE EYES IN BIGHTS OF LINE

A — SINGLE-HANDED SKIPPERS IN THE OLD DAYS HOISTED THEMSELVES ALOFT — POSSIBLE, EVEN PRACTICAL, BUT NOT RECOMMENDED

TWO DOUBLE-SHEAVE BLOCKS MECH. ADV. = 4× SECURED WITH TWO HALF-HITCHES IN THE BIGHT BROUGHT UP UNDER THE SUSPENDING HOOK BETWEEN THE STRAPS OF THE CHAIR

TWO HALF HITCHES IN THE BIGHT

D — A ROUND TURN AND A BOWLINE

A SHACKLE WITH ITS PIN MOUSED WITH WIRE

A DOUBLE-THREADED HALYARD SHACKLE

B — **E** — SAFETY IS THE PRIMARY CONCERN — ONE GOOD MATE ON THE JIB HALYARD WINCH, ANOTHER TAILING ON (KEEPING TENSION OVER THE WINCH DRUM) AND CLEATING THE HALYARD WHEN THE HEIGHT IS RIGHT

A SAFETY LINE KEEPS THE MATE ALOFT CLOSE TO THE MAST

JIB HALYARD

JIB HALYARD WINCH

TAILING ON

F — **G** — **H** — **I**

40

Going Aloft

Vertical voyages were easier in the days of square-rigged ships. The hands swarmed up into the rigging on ladder ropes called *ratlines*. But the trip was still dangerous. Knowing the engineering of line was termed *marlinespike seamanship*. Years of experience and many mistakes gave a small boat skipper the cautious confidence to hoist himself up the mast [**A**] for repairs.

Today, we can only substitute a passion for safety. A brave shipmate should be hoisted only in a well-made bosun's chair [**B**], which is made fast to the hoisting line with a *moused* hook (the mouth is safely lashed closed) [**C**], or another secure fastening [**D**]. The mate aloft should be kept close to the mast with a short safety line [**E**]. Friends on the deck can hoist the topside mate using the main or jib halyard with a winch [**F**], one cranking [**G**], one *tailing on* (keeping tension on the drum) [**H**]. If the angle to a *block* (pulley) aloft is good, an anchor winch with several turns on the winch drum can do the work [**I**] but the responsibility is heavier than the weight of the mate, and no distractions can interfere.

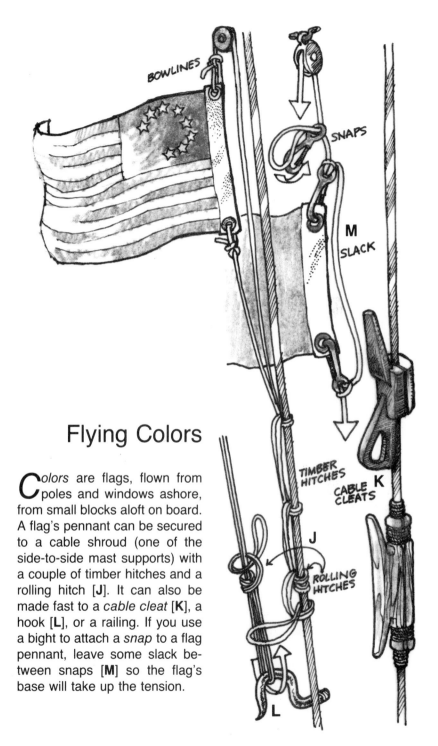

Flying Colors

Colors are flags, flown from poles and windows ashore, from small blocks aloft on board. A flag's pennant can be secured to a cable shroud (one of the side-to-side mast supports) with a couple of timber hitches and a rolling hitch [**J**]. It can also be made fast to a *cable cleat* [**K**], a hook [**L**], or a railing. If you use a bight to attach a *snap* to a flag pennant, leave some slack between snaps [**M**] so the flag's base will take up the tension.

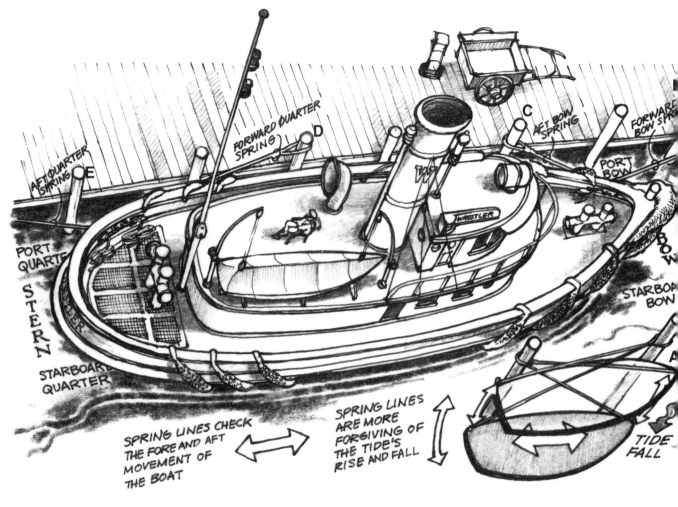

AFT QUARTER
SPRING E

FORWARD QUARTER
SPRING D

C AFT BOW
SPRING

FORWARD
BOW SPR

PORT
BOW

WRESTLER

PORT
QUARTER

STERN

STARBOARD
QUARTER

STARBOARD
BOW

BOW

SPRING LINES CHECK
THE FORE AND AFT
MOVEMENT OF
THE BOAT

SPRING LINES
ARE MORE
FORGIVING OF
THE TIDE'S
RISE AND FALL

TIDE
FALL

AFT QUARTER
SPRING

SPRINGING IN
FOR DOCKING   F

FORWARD
QUARTER SPRING

BACKING
ON A SPRING
FOR LEAVING   G

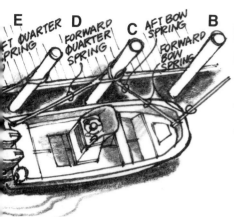

E AFT QUARTER SPRING D FORWARD QUARTER SPRING C AFT BOW SPRING B FORWARD BOW SPRING

AFT BOW SPRING FORWARD QUARTER SPRING

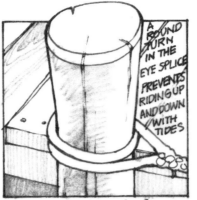

A ROUND TURN IN THE EYE SPLICE PREVENTS RIDING UP AND DOWN WITH TIDES

CLEAT CROSSINGS HALF HITCH

ROLLING HITCH

I

FENDERS

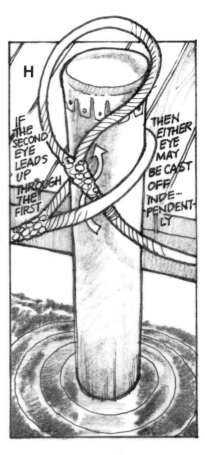

H

IF THE SECOND EYE LEADS UP THROUGH THE FIRST

THEN EITHER EYE MAY BE CAST OFF INDEPENDENTLY

Docklines

Boats don't rest, even when sailors do. They fret and strain at the dock, responding to the flow of the water.

Making a boat secure at a dock is part of marlinespike seamanship, and like much of line engineering, a matter of angles. *Spring lines* are docking lines that angle forward and aft. They are specifically named for their direction and the place where they are made fast on board: the *aft bow spring* runs aft from the bow. Because they are longer, spring lines respond better to tides; tying up a dinghy with a short bow line can leave it hanging when the tide falls ten or fifteen feet [A]. A boat of any size needs four springs: forward bow [B], aft bow [C], forward *quarter* (one side of the stern, or back) [D], aft quarter [E]. A spring's angle not only keeps a boat against the dock but parallel to it, and can help in maneuvering in [F] or out [G].

Generally, eye splices [H] or bowlines are dropped around dock pilings or bollards and the length of the springs are adjusted—and readjusted with the tide—from the boat's deck. Rubber or rope *fenders* [I] lie between the smooth hull and the rough dock.

43

Engineering a Button

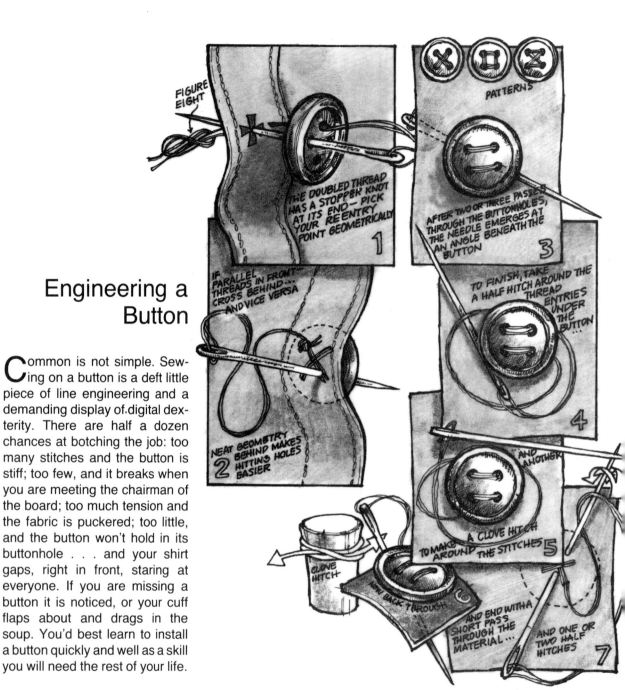

FIGURE EIGHT

THE DOUBLED THREAD HAS A STOPPER KNOT AT ITS END — PICK YOUR RE-ENTRY POINT GEOMETRICALLY **1**

IF PARALLEL THREADS IN FRONT CROSS BEHIND... ...AND VICE VERSA

NEAT GEOMETRY BEHIND MAKES HITTING HOLES EASIER **2**

PATTERNS

AFTER TWO OR THREE PASSES THROUGH THE BUTTONHOLES, THE NEEDLE EMERGES AT AN ANGLE BENEATH THE BUTTON **3**

TO FINISH, TAKE A HALF HITCH AROUND THE THREAD ENTRIES UNDER THE BUTTON... **4**

...AND ANOTHER

A CLOVE HITCH TO MAKE AROUND THE STITCHES **5**

CLOVE HITCH

AND BACK THROUGH

AND END WITH A SHORT PASS THROUGH THE MATERIAL...

AND ONE OR TWO HALF HITCHES **7**

Common is not simple. Sewing on a button is a deft little piece of line engineering and a demanding display of digital dexterity. There are half a dozen chances at botching the job: too many stitches and the button is stiff; too few, and it breaks when you are meeting the chairman of the board; too much tension and the fabric is puckered; too little, and the button won't hold in its buttonhole . . . and your shirt gaps, right in front, staring at everyone. If you are missing a button it is noticed, or your cuff flaps about and drags in the soup. You'd best learn to install a button quickly and well as a skill you will need the rest of your life.

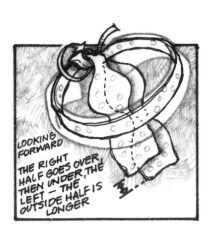

LOOKING FORWARD

THE RIGHT HALF GOES OVER, THEN UNDER, THE LEFT — THE OUTSIDE HALF IS LONGER

MAKE A BOW TO THE LEFT WITH THE INSIDE HALF, BENEATH THE OUTSIDE HALF — THE OUTSIDE HALF NOW SWINGS INSIDE, OVER THE FIRST BOW'S LEAD, AND MAKES A BOW TO THE RIGHT

PULL THE RIGHT BOW THROUGH — SHAPE AND FAIR BUT NOT TOO WELL — NEVER MAKE A BOW TIE PERFECTLY

Another life skill, for both women and men, is the tying of *ties*. Tying a bow tie is one of the great bugaboos of explanation, because it is so simple, so subtle. It is like explaining how to whistle. But if you arrange the tie neatly, as shown, with the outside bow hanging a little longer than the inside, then finding the standing part of the inside half-bow will not be difficult.

Police wear clip-on ties for the same reason that Alexander the Great had his soldiers cut their beards: to prevent assailants from grabbing them. You should not wear a clip-on.

Decorating a Neck

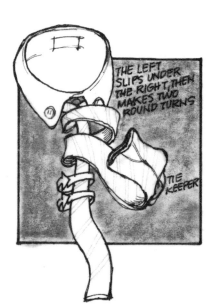

THE LEFT SLIPS UNDER THE RIGHT, THEN MAKES TWO ROUND TURNS

TIE KEEPER

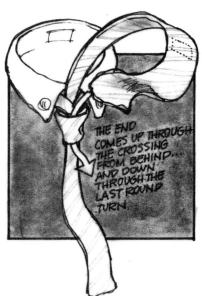

THE END COMES UP THROUGH THE CROSSING FROM BEHIND.... AND DOWN THROUGH THE LAST ROUND TURN.

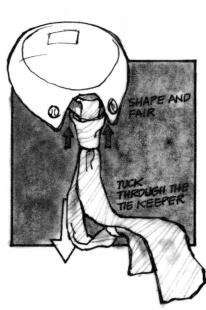

SHAPE AND FAIR

TUCK THROUGH THE TIE KEEPER

Hoisting a Dinghy

Although a faithful companion, the *dinghy* is a danger to itself and the boat it serves when the water gets rough. A well set-up boat will have chocks on the deckhouse [**A**] to accommodate its small friend, hard points at the dinghy's centerline [**B**], mount rings, and a cable harness [**C**]. The length of the harness legs are calculated for the dinghy's balance point. From a block near the masthead [**D**] lines drop to another block with a snap shackle. This clips into the harness [**E**], the dinghy is lifted, guided to its chocks, and turned as it is lowered, so its *gunwales* (outer edges) rest on one set of chocks. The block and tackle is unclipped and the dinghy is lowered upside down onto the other side's chocks [**F**]. Lashed across and diagonally [**G**], the dinghy is secure.

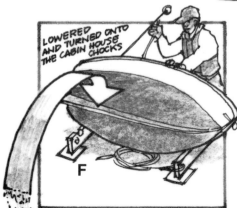

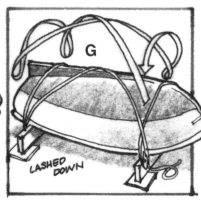

Securing a Hat

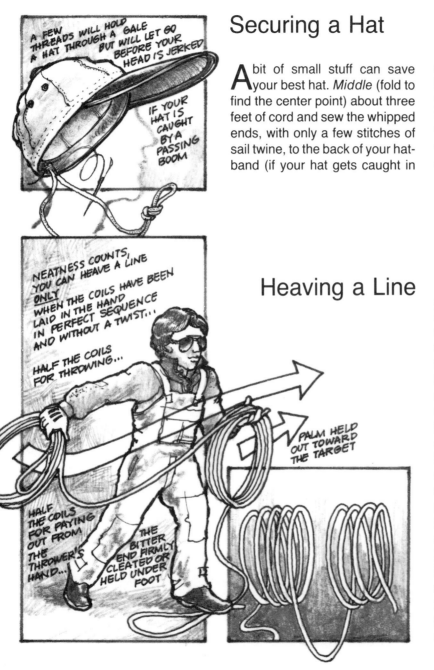

A bit of small stuff can save your best hat. *Middle* (fold to find the center point) about three feet of cord and sew the whipped ends, with only a few stitches of sail twine, to the back of your hatband (if your hat gets caught in something, you don't want your hat loop to drag you off and hang you). Pass the loop over your head before you put the hat on. With the connections at the back, you won't lose the hat to wind or gravity, frontward or backward.

A FEW THREADS WILL HOLD A HAT THROUGH A GALE BUT WILL LET GO BEFORE YOUR HEAD IS JERKED

IF YOUR HAT IS CAUGHT BY A PASSING BOOM

Heaving a Line

A critical time is often upon you when you need to throw a line from one place to another. In almost all critical times you should slow down a little. The success of heaving a line rests solely in the neat, sequential order of the coils you *lay up*— slowly and carefully. Lay them up in one hand and take half the coils, in order, with the other. The bitter end on your side should be secured somewhere or held under your foot. Point your outstretched palm toward your target and heave the line with an even, easy stroke. Don't try too hard. The weight of the coil in flight should carry it on and should strip the coils from your palm. The critical moment would go easier if you had practiced this a few times.

NEATNESS COUNTS, YOU CAN HEAVE A LINE ONLY WHEN THE COILS HAVE BEEN LAID IN THE HAND IN PERFECT SEQUENCE AND WITHOUT A TWIST...

HALF THE COILS FOR THROWING...

PALM HELD OUT TOWARD THE TARGET

HALF THE COILS FOR PAYING OUT FROM THE THROWER'S HAND...

THE BITTER END FIRMLY CLEATED OR HELD UNDER FOOT

INDEX

This book had a long gestation over a troubled time but the subject is part of me and stayed bright. The drawings were done in ink and pencil on heavy vellum and on linen-finish board. The manuscript was composed on XyWrite, transferred in the traditional hard copy, and was warred over with time-honored slips and blue pencils. It was set in Helvetica with Helvetica titles and printed and bound by Arcata Graphics/Hawkins.

The granddaddy knotsman was Clifford W. Ashley, who wrote the great *Ashley Book of Knots*. I met Mrs. Ashley many years after her husband's death and told her of my respect for Ashley's perseverance. She ventured that she never wanted to see another knot. I still have a few in me.

Thanks to my board of advisors:

Alban Adkins, roofer and father
Roy Andersen, whoopie tie yi yo
Dr. Paula Butterfield, pirate
Dr. Matthew Finn, marsh warden
Sgt. Pat Gavin, former Road Dog
Otto Kurz, black gang
Neil Leva, colonel of comfort
Dr. Frank Pisciotta, mean forehand
Sarah Risher, gonzo sage
  consultant
Steve Sperry, fighter pilot and
  sailmaker
Matthew and Martha Stackpole,
  islanders
Dr. Judith Walker, fit to be tied